African American History
Reconstruction

By Jennifer Howse

Published by Weigl Publishers Inc.
350 5th Avenue, Suite 3304, PMB 6G
New York, NY 10118-0069

Website: www.weigl.com
Copyright ©2009 WEIGL PUBLISHERS INC.

All of the Internet URLs given in the book were valid at the time of publication. However, due to the dynamic nature of the Internet, some addresses may have changed, or sites may have ceased to exist since publication. While the author and publisher regret any inconvenience this may cause readers, no responsibility for any such changes can be accepted by either the author or the publisher.

Library of Congress Cataloging-in-Publication Data available upon request.
Fax 1-866-44-WEIGL for the attention of the Publishing Records department.

ISBN 978-1-59036-878-7 (hard cover)
ISBN 978-1-59036-879-4 (soft cover)

Printed in the United States of America
1 2 3 4 5 6 7 8 9 0 12 11 10 09 08

Weigl acknowledges Getty Images as its primary image supplier for this title.

Every reasonable effort has been made to trace ownership and to obtain permission to reprint copyright material. The publishers would be pleased to have any errors or omissions brought to their attention so that they may be corrected in subsequent printings.

Editor: Heather C. Hudak
Designer: Terry Paulhus

Contents

5   A Question
    of Freedom

6   Slavery and
    Abolitionists

9   Civil War

10 Gaining the Right
    to Fight

12 Constitutional
    Amendments

14 Life as a Freed Slave

17 Frances Ellen
    Watkins Harper

18 Building a
    New Society

20 Redefining
    Citizenship

22 Exodus

24 Education

26 Southern Resistance

28 Life as a Citizen

30 Eroding Freedoms

32 Crime and
    Punishment

34 Jim Crow Laws

36 End of the Dream

38 Tunis Campbell

40 A New Hope

42 Timeline

44 Activity

45 Test Your Knowledge

46 Further Research

47 Glossary

48 Index

FREEDOM FOR ALL, BOTH BLACK AND WHITE!

A Question of Freedom

The struggle to end slavery defined the nineteenth century in the United States. In the late 1800s, the **democratic** government, and the people, of the United States were growing uncomfortable with the practice of enslaving part of the population. By 1860, the **Union** was in turmoil. The southern states that supported slavery took a stand against the northern states. In protest, 11 southern states separated from the Union, and set up a territorial government they called the Confederacy. The issue of slavery was at the core of the conflict. The quest to end slavery eventually started a war between the Union and the **Confederate** states. Thousands of people died in the conflict, called the Civil War. Yet, the war would eventually bring about an end to slavery. When the war ended the United States began to create a new vision for the country. This time was known as the Reconstruction period.

On June 19, 1865, two months after the end of the Civil War, the last slaves received the news that they were free. President Abraham Lincoln offered **amnesty** to all southerners of European ancestry who were willing to take an oath of loyalty to the Union. However, soon after, President Lincoln was **assassinated** and a new government formed under President Andrew Johnson.

During the Reconstruction years of 1866 to 1876, the Constitution of the United States was changed to ensure freedom for African Americans. The South needed a plan of action to re-build after the war, and freed people needed to learn how to live within the new societal order. This was an era of intense social, political, and economic change faced by Americans after the damage of the Civil War.

General Robert E. Lee was an important military advisor to Confederate leader Jefferson Davis.

TECHNOLOGY LINK
Learn more about the lives of African Americans who lived during the time of the Reconstruction at **http://lcweb4.loc.gov/ammem/asp**.

Slavery and Abolitionists

In 1860, more than 385,000 people in the United States owned slaves.

Africans were first brought to the United States in the 1600s as indentured laborers. However, the demand for cheap labor grew, and out of that need, life-long slavery was instituted. Supporters of slavery argued that African Americans were only suited to a life of service, and were incapable of learning to work or live independently. Over the next 300 years, **abolitionists** fought for the freedoms and civil liberties of African Americans. In 1820, they won a victory that outlawed the trans-Atlantic slave trade. This slowed the practice of kidnapping and transporting Africans for the purpose of selling them into slavery in North and South America.

Roots of Slavery

Using slave labor to grow and sell crops was a highly profitable method of operating a plantation, or farm. The economies of the southern states, such as Virginia, Georgia, Alabama, Louisiana, and South Carolina, developed rapidly with the use of slave labor. After the invention of the cotton gin in 1793, cotton became the main money-making crop in the South. The need for a cheap labor to grow and pick cotton increase, and slaves became an important part of this economy.

Racism as an Institution

Over time, slavery became an acceptable part of society, and it was enforced by severe laws and punishments. In the nineteenth century, the first step toward freedom for African Americans was to end slavery as an **institution**. The next step, eliminating **racism** from the culture, was much more difficult.

Few slave families were able to stay together. Children and spouses were often sold to other plantations.

Lincoln the President

Civil War

In 1860, the Republican candidate, Abraham Lincoln, was elected President of the United States. He won the presidency in part because he campaigned with a promise to **abolish** slavery. Many people in the southern states felt that President Lincoln was a threat to their right to own slaves. They believed that the economy, and their incomes, relied on slave labor.

The South Rises Against the North

The Confederacy wanted to take over all government responsibilities and military buildings within their newly established borders. The Union government of the northern states refused to turn over the military forts within the Confederate borders. In retaliation, a Confederate army was raised.

On April 12, 1861, the Confederates attacked Fort Sumter, a federal stronghold in Charleston, South Carolina. The Confederate army won the battle. The fort was surrendered to them, and the Civil War began.

African Americans Excluded from the Fight

At the outbreak of war, free African Americans tried to enlist in the army. They wanted to fight for the end of slavery and prove their loyalty to the Union. However, Lincoln did not endorse African Americans fighting as equals in army. He believed that allowing African Americans to join the Union army might offend the Confederate states. He hoped that tensions would subside and a peaceful resolution could be reached.

Gettysburg Address

On November 19, 1863, the Civil War had claimed thousands of lives, and in an effort to strengthen support from the public to continue the fight, Abraham Lincoln gave a speech at a memorial to the battle at Gettysburg, Pennsylvania, Lincoln spoke:

"Four score and seven years ago our fathers brought forth on this continent, a new nation, conceived in **Liberty**, and dedicated to the proposition that all men are created equal. Now we are engaged in a great civil war, testing whether that nation, or any nation so conceived and so dedicated, can long endure. … the world will little note, nor long remember what we say here, but it can never forget what they did here. … from these honored dead we take increased devotion to that cause for which they gave the last full measure of devotion that we here highly resolve that these dead shall not have died in vain that this nation, under God, shall have a new birth of freedom and that government of the people, by the people, for the people, shall not perish from the earth."

Gaining the Right to Fight

The war did not end, and thousands of soldiers died on both sides of the conflict. The urgent need for more soldiers to continue to fight was answered when two acts of **Congress** were passed on July 17, 1862. These acts allowed African Americans to the join Union Army.

As many as 2.5 million men served in the Union army during the Civil War.

African American men rushed to enlist, but the acts only applied to men who were free before the war started. This created a sharp division between African American communities. To correct this imbalance President Lincoln announced the Emancipation Proclamation on January 1, 1863. According to the proclamation, all slaves in areas that were rebelling against the federal government would be freed. The proclamation also stated that the Union was ready to accept African American recruits into its army.

First Steps

African American leader, scholar, and educator Frederick Douglass stated that the Emancipation Proclamation was the first step toward freedom. Yet, the proclamation was limited because it only applied to states that had separated from the Union. States, such as Kentucky and Delaware, that were loyal to the Union but bordered between the North and the South still allowed the practice of slavery. The proclamation also said the end of slavery would only come into effect if the Union won the war.

At the end of the Civil War, many African Americans, including men, women, and children began learning to read and write.

Gathering Armies

African American abolitionists worked to end slavery, and their supporters went on recruitment drives in the North. They encouraged African American men to join the Union army. Though the Emancipation Proclamation had freed all slaves, the Confederacy continued to fight for the right to enslave African Americans. Abolitionists believed that African Americans should play a part in securing their own freedom and claiming equal **citizenship**.

A New Vision

Following the Civil War, the Reconstruction era began. Reconstruction was seen as an opportunity to create a society that did not discriminate against its citizens based on race. During the war, the nation saw the end of slavery and tried to define the meaning of freedom.

By the end of the war it was clear that Reconstruction would bring far-reaching changes to the nation, especially in the southern states. Freedom for African Americans meant freedom from control and oppression. This came in many forms, such as re-uniting with families and communities that slavery had forced apart. African Americans built schools and churches, and took part in government. Having their freedoms allowed African Americans to earn wages and have certain **civil rights**. However, this transition demanded a new relationship between people of European ancestry and African Americans. As a result, during Reconstruction racism was common in all areas of the United States.

Constitutional Amendments

The Emancipation Proclamation was a first step toward ending the practice of slavery in the United States. In response, the Confederate government introduced new laws called Black Codes. The codes outlined the kinds of jobs open to African Americans. They could only work on farms or as housekeepers. In some places, African Americans had to apply to a justice of the peace to work in a job other than farming. Under the Black Codes, growing crops African Americans could sell was also discouraged, as was the ability to move freely and live where they chose. African Americans were barred from living in cities and towns, and short visits to these places were monitored by lawmakers.

Establishing Civil Rights

During the Reconstruction period, Congress passed two laws and three constitutional **amendments** that gave African Americans rights. The Black Codes were eliminated with the passage of the Civil Rights Act of 1866. The act gave African Americans rights and privileges of full citizenship. Constitutional amendments thirteen, fourteen, and fifteen are called the Reconstruction amendments. They were passed after the Civil War to address the status of African Americans. The amendments

African Americans and abolitionists held a celebration in Washington, DC, to commemorate the Thirteenth Amendment, which outlawed slavery.

were the national government's response to the Black Codes.

Thirteenth Amendment

In 1865, the Thirteenth Amendment outlawed the practice of slavery, saying it was against a person's civil rights. This amendment freed slaves across the United States without limitation.

According to the amendment, no person could be forced into slavery any place in the United States unless they had been given this punishment as a sentence for a crime.

Fourteenth Amendment

The Fourteenth Amendment tried to give African Americans equal protection under the law. They would be counted as members of the population and have equal government representation. The amendment also stated that government representatives who fought in support of the Confederate states could only take office if they received two thirds of Congress' votes. A former Confederate state could only be admitted to the Union after the state **ratified** the Fourteenth Amendment within its state. All of the states refused, with the exception of Tennessee. However, by 1870, the remaining 10 Confederate states ratified the amendment.

Fifteenth Amendment

The Fifteenth Amendment extended the right to vote to African American men. Still, some southern states added clauses to their state constitutions that made it difficult for African Americans to vote. These clauses often stated that only citizens who had the right to vote prior to 1866 or 1867 could vote in an election.

Frederick Douglass

In 1865, African American leader Frederick Douglass said that African Americans would only be free from slavery when they had earned the right to vote. Douglass was an educator, abolitionist, and civil rights advocate during the Civil War and Reconstruction period. An advisor to Lincoln, Douglass lobbied for all three of the constitutional amendments that were ratified by 1870.

At the age of 23 in 1841, Douglass spoke for the first time before an audience of abolitionists. He continued to lecture throughout his life about ending slavery, earning rights for African Americans, and helping women obtain the right to vote. In the Reconstruction era, Douglass spoke out against the Black Codes and the **lynching** of African Americans.

Frederick Douglass died on February 20, 1895. He left behind a legacy as a great African American leader who contributed to the Constitution of the United States and helped secure equal rights for all people.

Life as a Freed Slave

The concept of freedom was hard to grasp for people who had been slaves throughout their lives.

Former slave Joseph Holmes was born in Henry County, Virginia, in 1856. He recalled that his slave owner did not allow her slaves to be mistreated. She was a trader in the slave market and was concerned for her property. Holmes said that it took many years before he fully understood what his mistress meant when she told him he was free.

"…Miss tole us us wuz free but hit wuz ten or twelve years atter de Surrender befo' I railly knowed whut she meant. I wuz a big boy goin' tuh school afore I had any understandin' as tuh whut she meant."

Another former slave, Charles Graham, had vivid memories of learning about his freedom.

"I got a chance to see the troops after the civil war was over… The first clear thing I remember was when everybody was rejoicing because they were free. I was too young to pay much attention, but they were cutting up and clapping their hands and carrying on something terrible and shouting Free, Free, old Abraham done turned us loose.

"Some of the slaves went right up north. We stayed in Clarksville and worked there for a year or two. In 1864, we went to Warren County, Illinois. They put me in school. My people were just common laborers. They bought themselves a nice little home."

Graham's father had escaped before the Civil War, and his mother was ill. He joined his uncle's family in their **migration** to Illinois. Families joined together or fell apart as African Americans had the freedom to move and create new lives for themselves.

Quick Facts

The 1860 **census** reported the total population of the United States as 31,443,790. Of this number, 14.1 percent, or 4,441,790, were African American.

According to official records, runaway slaves numbered 1,011, but by 1850, the actual number was believed to be closer to 7,000.

The post-Civil War migration north involved a shift of the African American population from southern agricultural regions to cities in the northern states.

In 1850, the total free population in the fifteen eastern states was 212,814. By 1890, it had increased to 505,315.

Frances Ellen Watkins Harper

Born to free parents, Frances Ellen Watkins Harper made it her life's work to secure the civil rights of African Americans. Through her writing and poetry, Frances spread the word of abolition and **enfranchisement**.

Early Beginnings
Frances was born in Baltimore, Maryland, on September 24, 1825. Her mother died when she was only three years old. Frances went to live with her mother's brother, William J. Watkins, who was an abolitionist and advocate of civil rights.

Frances was educated at her uncle's school, the Academy for Negro Youth. Her first job was as a servant at the home of a **Quaker** family who had a large library. This family urged Frances to use the library, and she began writing. Her poems were accepted for newspapers, and in 1845, her collection of poems, *Autumn Leaves*, was published.

In 1850, the **Fugitive** Slave law was passed, restricting the movement of African Americans. Frances fled to Pennsylvania in 1851. She began helping slaves escape to Canada along the Underground Railroad.

Quakers are peaceful people who do not believe in war. Many Quakers were active abolitionists.

Writing the Reconstruction
Frances believed change could only come when all people had the right to vote and equal representation in the government. The first of Frances' protest poems were published in 1854. Entitled *Poems on Miscellaneous Subjects*, these poems attacked racism and the oppression of women. Part of the money she earned from her poems was used to help slaves escape.

Frances began lecturing about education and the ideals of Reconstruction at public gatherings. One of her best-known speeches was before the National Women's Rights Convention in 1866. She demanded equal rights for all women. Another collection of poems was printed in 1872. Entitled *Sketches of Southern Life*, were told through the voice of a former slave living in the southern states during Reconstruction. Frances then wrote two novels, *Sowing and Reaping* and *Trial and Triumph*.

In 1873, Frances was appointed as Superintendent of the Colored Section of the Philadelphia and Pennsylvania Women's Christian Temperance Union. Frances died of heart disease on February 22, 1911, at the age of 86.

Building a New Society

The last battle of the Civil War was the fall of Richmond, Virginia, on April 2, 1865. The city was destroyed by fire and riots. By April 9, the Civil War was over. Losses among African Americans were high. About one-third of all African Americans enrolled in the military lost their lives during.

National Crisis

The Confederate states were devastated by the Civil War, which created a national crisis. Economies were in ruin, as were farms across the South. Former slaves had to learn how to live with their freedom, as well as find and keep employment.

The Union army disbanded, cutting the number of troops in the South from one million to 152,000 by the end of 1865. Over the next five years, many former slaves began to move to southern towns and cities.

The Reconstruction Act of 1867 was the federal government's plan to establish order in the South and help freed African Americans. One of the key elements of the plan was the Freedmen's Bureau.

Freedmen's Bureau

The former slave states were divided into five military districts, and an assistant commissioner was appointed to each district. By 1868, the Refugees, Freedmen, and Abandoned Lands, also known as the Freedmen's Bureau, was established. Bureau representatives were placed

The Freedmen's Bureau's greatest success was helping establish as many as 3,000 schools for freed slaves.

throughout the South to enforce the Reconstruction order and protect former slaves. The main goals of the Bureau were to provide food, medical care, help with resettlement, manage abandoned property, regulate labor, and establish schools for African Americans. The Bureau also enacted laws, collected taxes, administered punishment for crimes, and used military force. In effect, the Bureau became the local government.

Opposition

Reconstruction was started by President Lincoln, but his successor, Andrew Johnson, did not support the plan. As well, the Bureau was not able to resolve many issues in the South, particularly, land management.

Although, the initial plan awarded 850,000 acres of land to freedmen, President Johnson returned the land to its Confederate owners. The focus was then placed on finding employment for freedmen, who were encouraged to work on plantations. The lack of funding from the government halted the reach of the Bureau, and by 1869, Congress shut it down.

Charitable organizations offered assistance to freedmen including the American Missionary Association, the National Freemen's Relief Association, the American Freedmen's Union, and the Western Freedmen's Aid Commission. About 50 charities provided food, clothing, money, books, and teachers.

Quick Facts

Healthcare was an important function of the Freedmen's Bureau. More than 500,000 patients were treated by Bureau physicians and surgeons. Sixty health facilities were established.

About 30,000 men were transported from refugee and relief stations to farms. Strict rules were placed on employers and laborers. The laborers were free to choose who they worked for, and there could be no fixed wages or forced labor.

Redefining Citizenship

Freedom in a democratic society includes the right to vote and to be represented by the government. Extending democracy to include African American men was passed in the Fifteenth Amendment to the United States Constitution, on March 30, 1870. This amendment stated that all male citizens were entitled to vote, and that race was no longer a barrier to voting.

Finding a Political Voice

For the first time, African Americans voted, and sent representatives to the United States Congress. Over the previous 20 years of political conflicts, many were directly related to African Americans and their place in American society. Widespread and different interest in politics became part of African American communities. In certain southern states, where there was a large population of African Americans they held greater political power. African American delegates attended state constitutional conventions, and African American state legislators were voted into office.

The Fifteenth Amendment states that no man can be denied the right to vote based on race, color, or previous condition of servitude.

The constitutional conventions wrote new laws and abolished the Black Codes. Two African Americans served in the Senate and 20 served as House Representatives.

African American Conventions

African Americans became involved in the political process as voters and as government representatives at the local, state, and national level. Although their elections were often challenged by people of European ancestry, many African American men served in government during Reconstruction. Interest in politics grew, and by 1865, hundreds of delegates were attending African American conventions in the southern states.

In 1869, the National Convention of Colored Men fought for equal rights and spoke out against violence toward African Americans. The main focus of the convention was to inquire into the actual condition of African Americans in the United States. A committee was formed to address this issue, and President Ulysses S. Grant endorsed the work of the committee. The president also pledged equal protection under the law.

Reverend Hiram Revels

Mississippi Republican senator Reverend Hiram Revels was the first African American elected to the United States Senate. Revels was born in North Carolina n 1822 to free parents. He worked as a barber and a minister in the African Methodist Episcopal Church.

During the Civil War, Revels served as an army chaplain. After the war, he won his first political office of alderman in 1868. Then, he successfully ran for the state senate in 1870. Some senators objected to Revels taking the office of senator, arguing that he was not a citizen for a period of nine years before he was elected, a requirement

for serving in the senate. This obstacle was overcome when the senate voted 48 to 8 in favor allowing Revels to take office. He served from February 25, 1870, to March 4, 1881.

After his term in office, Hiram was appointed president of the Alcorn University, the first land-grant college for African American students. Revels died January 16, 1901. Nearly 100 years passed before another African American was elected to the Senate. From 1967 to 1979, Republican Edward Brooke of Massachusetts served in the Senate. The first African American woman elected to the Senate was Carol Moseley-Braun. She served from 1993 to 1999.

Exodus

During the period before the Emancipation Proclamation, fugitive slaves fled from areas that allowed slavery. They had to leave the southern states in order to find safety and freedom. After the Civil War, African Americans left the southern states seeking a new life, employment, and to re-unite with family members that slavery had torn apart. Large numbers of African Americans moved to the northern states.

Kansas
Tens of thousands of African Americans left the southern states and went to Kansas. Fugitives moved in great numbers to permanent African American settlements, such as Nicodemus. This was one of 20 towns created to offer permanent

residence to African Americans. In 1850, the African American population of the town was listed as zero. By 1890, the population was 49,710.

Supported by abolitionist societies, such as the Kansas Emancipation League, African Americans created **self-sufficient** communities. The movement began to fade by 1881.

Canada

For decades prior to Reconstruction, runaway slaves had fled to Canada. Canada was a commonwealth country of Great Britain, which had outlawed slavery in 1772. Therefore, any slave who reached Canada was considered free.

Over a period 30 years as many as 2,000 African Americans entered Canada each year. Most settled in Ontario in cities such as Toronto, Chatham, London, and Windsor. All-African American communities developed, such as Dawn, Dresden, Wilberforce, and Buxton. About 30,000 fugitives lived in Canada by the beginning of the Civil War.

Africa

Supported by charitable societies, African Americans migrated to colonies in Liberia, Africa. Some African Americans believed that they would never have equality in the United States, and they sought a self-governing state in Africa.

The first known **colonization** effort was in Sierra Leone, Liberia. The American Colonization Society supported colonies where African Americans attempted to achieve a sense of freedom and liberty.

Haiti, West Indies, and Mexico

Many African Americans did not agree with the philosophy of the American Colonization Society. They moved to other areas, such as Haiti, West Indies, and Mexico. Haiti actively sought immigrants from the nearby United States. To ease the labor shortage, Haiti offered free land to immigrants. Between 8,000 to 13,000 African Americans migrated to Haiti. However, most of the African Americans who went to Haiti or the West Indies eventually returned to the United States.

Quick Facts

A person's race was recorded as part of the information gathered by census takers in 1870. From this information, the migration patterns of African Americans are traced. Maps were produced from 1870 to 1920 to demonstrate this movement.

An atlas published with information from the 1890 census shows the percentage of African Americans within each county. This atlas also shows the areas with the fastest African American population growth were New York City, Philadelphia, Pittsburgh, Cleveland, Toledo, and Chicago.

Education

Before the Civil War, only about 10 to 15 percent of African Americans in the South were literate. Teaching a slave how to read and write was illegal. An educated slave was considered prone to rebellion. The Reconstruction plan made access to education a priority.

Providing education for freed slaves was one of the main functions of the Freedmen's Bureau. It built state run schools, employed teachers, and supplied books throughout the South. Other organizations, such as the American Missionary Society, and churches also started schools and colleges. More than 1,000 schools were built, teacher-training institutions were created, and colleges were founded.

The conditions that many African Americans faced as slaves did not prepare them for life after the Civil War. The question of whether the education of African Americans should focus upon practical training, such as building or farming, or the liberal arts became the focus of discussions among African American leaders. To many leaders of European

As well as teaching students to read and write, many schools offered practical training, such as construction, to young African Americans.

ancestry, providing practical education meant African Americans would continue to work as housekeepers and laborers.

Tuskegee Institute

The Tuskegee Institute was founded in 1871. It offered training in agriculture, domestic science, and manual and industrial arts. The courses developed at Tuskegee served as models, not just in the U.S., but in nations all over the developing world.

Spelman College

Founded in 1881, Spelman was the first independent African American college for women. The first students graduated from Spelman in 1887.

Howard University

Founded in 1867, Howard University educated freedmen. Located in Washington, DC, it offered faculties of law, pharmacy, medicine, theology, dentistry, music, engineering, and architecture. Today, the university is open to all qualified students, but it remains a mainly African American institute.

End of the Bureau

When the Freedmen's Bureau was closed, education initiatives stopped. Still, schools continued to produce graduates. African American communities started schools and maintained them with local resources.

New Orleans Tribune

One of the voices of African Americans was the *New Orleans Tribune*. On October 4, 1864, it became the first daily newspaper produced by African Americans. The *Tribune* was created by Louis Charles Roudanez, an African American doctor born June 12, 1823.

Roudanez and a small group of African Americans created two newspapers to promote African American rights. *L'Union* was the first African American owned newspaper in the South. Opposition to the paper caused it closure in 1864.

Roudanez wanted to continue to provide a voice for the African American community. He started *La Tribune de la Nouvelle Orleans*. Though the newspaper went bankrupt its legacy continues today as a political **periodical**.

Southern Resistance

African Americans were unsure of how ready members of their community were to embrace civil liberties. The transition from slave to government representative was difficult. People struggled to become literate and self-sufficient. Guidance came from the church, ministers, and community leaders.

Political Opposition

In 1877, federal troops withdrew from the South. Neither the troops or the Freedmen's Bureau were able to support or protect African Americans. Reconstruction gains in equality, the right to vote, and government participation stopped by the end of 1877, and African Americans were subjected to a lesser form of citizenship.

Economic Struggle

The efforts of the Freedmen's Bureau toward establishing freed slaves as landowners did not succeed. President Lincoln's Reconstruction plan called for abandoned plantations be granted to former slaves after the Civil War. The freedmen could plant their own crops and develop self-sufficient

economies. However, President Johnson turned the land back over to former slave owners.

To secure the labor of the freed slaves, a new type of economy formed. **Sharecrop** farms were sectioned off and former slaves signed agreements to work the land. However, these agreements were designed to keep African Americans poor and powerless.

Social Confrontation

Generations of slave trade had supported the myth that African Americans were best suited to work as laborers. This idea was deeply rooted in American society, and it became a way of life. Laws, religious practices, and social customs, were established and maintained by the ruling class. Despite the losses from the Civil War, the ruling class wanted to maintain this way of life. Although Reconstruction was offered as a way to erase the Black Codes and ease the transition to freedom for African Americans, racism and **segregation** remained in southern society.

Freed slaves continued to face many hardships. Opportunities were limited, so many African Americans struggled to find work, homes, and enough money to feed their families

Life as a Citizen

Martin Delany, a free-born African American, worked as a surgeon in the Union army.

Freedom was a new concept for former slaves. As the Union army conquered the South, many slaves fled the area. These freed people faced new problems. They had no place to live or work. The histories of African Americans during these times are recorded in diaries and letters. One such diary is that of Houston Hartsfield Holloway, who described his experiences in Meriwether and Pike Counties, Georgia. The diary spans Holloway's life as a slave, as a blacksmith during the Civil War, and as an minister during Reconstruction. More than a daily account of activities, Holloway's diary also contains work songs, hymns, and cultural symbols.

"For we colored people did not know how to be free and the white people did not know how to have a free colored person about them," Holloway wrote.

In addition to diaries, African Americans expressed themselves through speeches. People spread the word of Reconstruction and debated its aims. Some African American leaders, such as Major Martin R. Delany, returned to the South.

After a respected career in the Union army, Delany began working for the Freedmen's Bureau. He called for freed African Americans to become landowners, but his ideas were considered radical, and he was removed from his post by 1865.

Although Major Delany's attempts to gain a political office failed, he continued to speak at gatherings about embracing African Americans' freedom and becoming a self-sufficient and independent. Delany wrote many newspaper and magazine articles and published several books.

Written and spoken words record the history of Reconstruction. Music and song were powerful methods of spreading the word of freedom. The songs *No More Auction Block for Me*, or *Many Thousand Gone* were published in 1869. They outlines how freed slaves would no longer be auctioned off at market for slave owners to buy.

The African American Church

Churches often served as the core of the community. Religion was a way of understanding issues related to race, slavery, and abolition. African American ministers preached that emancipation was God's plan. Churches were seen as religious centers, and also political places where the issues of civil liberties were praised. Schools were established in church halls or basements, and church buildings were used as meeting places for special interest groups.

In 1867, Reverend John Jasper, a former slave, began his ministry at Sixth Mount Zion in an abandoned Confederate horse stable in Richmond, Virginia. John became known nationally as an **orator**, and led his congregation through difficult times during and after Reconstruction.

The First African Baptist Church in Lexington, Kentucky, was founded in 1790 and rebuilt during the Reconstruction period in 1856. This church is the oldest African Baptist Church in Kentucky and the third oldest in the United States. The funeral of Peter "Old Captain" Durrett, the church's first minister, is said to have been one of the largest funerals ever held in Lexington.

Eroding Freedoms

During Reconstruction, amazing gains were made for African Americans. They were liberated from slavery, fought for their freedom as members of the Union army, and gained the right to vote. These were tremendous advancements towards equality and citizenship. However, near the end of the Reconstruction period, from about 1877 to 1900, former slave owners and supporters of the Confederate states united against what they viewed as the threat of African American liberty. The political, economic, and social power that was beginning to develop in African American communities was considered defiant and out of control. Some southerners wanted to reinstate the ruling class.

Slave Labor

By 1865, the same year the Black Codes were written, President Johnson began a campaign to return power back to the Southern elite. These laws were the first attempt to return African Americans to the conditions they lived under before emancipation. The Black Codes were quickly struck down by the Thirteenth, Fourteenth, and Fifteenth Amendments of the United States Constitution. Yet, controls on African Americans still existed on a local level.

For example, local laws restricted freedom of movement for African Americans. This was an attempt to control the labor force. Jobs open to African Americans were limited, and if they refused to sign labor contracts, they were punished or their children were taken away.

Election Violence

Southerners of European ancestry opposed African Americans participating in the election process. To protest, mass numbers of people of European ancestry voted to ensure their candidates were elected. In some cases, they took the opposite approach, refusing to cast any ballots. In the event that these two actions failed to sway the political elections, they used violence and intimidation to prevent African Americans from voting. In 1867 in Calhoun, Georgia, a group of African Americans faced violence and threats, so they petitioned the federal government to send troops to elections.

Denied the Right to Vote

The Fifteenth Amendment was redefined by individual states. State legislatures passed discriminatory laws by creating new requirements for voter registration. During the period of 1890 to 1908, 11 states enacted new constitutions or amendments to state constitutions that required voters to pay a **pole tax**, pass a literacy test, or meet residency rules. Under these new laws, hundreds of thousands of African Americans could not vote.

The right to vote was taken away from many African Americans. Without political power, African American voters could not elect representatives to Congress or the Senate.

African Americans had great hope for equality with the passing of the Fifteenth Amendment.

CELEBRATION AT BALTIMORE ON MAY 19th 1870.

THE FIFTEENTH AMENDMENT AND ITS RESULTS.

Respectfully dedicated to the colored Citizens of the U S of America A.D.1870. by Schneider & Fuchs. 184 N.Eutaw St. Baltimore Md.

Crime and Punishment

A terrorist group formed in the Southern states, and its beliefs spread throughout the country. Violence and intimidation used against African Americans and their supporters ended Reconstruction in the South. Born out of fear, the Ku Klux Klan (KKK) gained power when local governments were weakened after the Civil War. Their activities included civil disobedience, **vigilantism**, and patrolling areas with firearms. KKK groups formed in many communities across the South.

Highly secretive, these **paramilitary** groups tried to scare people. If this approach did not work, they would terrorize victims with whippings, hangings, and lynchings. The purpose of these acts was to warn others not to rise up against **supremacist** groups. Crimes were committed against African Americans and others who supported the quest for civil rights.

Violence against African Americans continued to grow. In October 1869, African American Georgia legislator Abram Colby was kidnapped and whipped by political opponents. In 1871, Abram stood before Congress and described the crimes against him. President Ulysses Grant pushed for a stop to the violence in South.

Whipping was used to frighten and intimidate African Americans.

Quick Facts

From May 1 to 3, 1866, civilians and police of European ancestry rioted and killed 46 African Americans. Several other people were injured, and many homes, churches, and schools were destroyed. Known as the Memphis Massacre, this was part of the violence meant to control African American populations.

In New Orleans, on July 30, 1866, police raided a **suffrage** meeting of African Americans and their Republican supporters. Forty people were killed and 150 injured.

The Colfax Massacre occurred on April 13, 1869. The White League battled with state militia that was made up of mostly African American soldiers. More than 100 African Americans die.

Jim Crow Laws

Despite the civil liberties gained by African Americans throughout the Reconstruction period, by 1877, another form of control was enacted. Black Laws, or Jim Crow laws were passed in several southern states. These laws legalized segregation by removing civil liberties from African Americans based upon their race.

Restrictions on Public Life

African Americans were restricted in their use of public facilities, such as schools, churches, public transport, and water fountains. They could only use facilities designated for African Americans. Laws also prevented adult African American men from voting. In every state of the former Confederacy, a system of legalized segregation was fully in place by 1910.

Restrictions on Movement

The ability for African Americans to move freely and live where they chose was also limited under the Jim Crow laws. African Americans were barred from living in cities and towns, and short visits to these places were monitored by lawmakers. Passes were required to move from one place to another. This proved to be a means of controlling African Americans ability to move

The Jim Crow laws required African American children to attend segregated schools.

from place to place but also to prevent them from seeking better living conditions or employment.

Enforcing Restrictions

Within towns and cities, there were strict laws passed as an attempt to control migrants or homeless African Americans. Large numbers of people left rural areas to find work in cities. In Mississippi, for example, the "pig law" made stealing a pig an act of grand larceny. The punishment was five years in jail. As a result of this

In the 1950s, African Americans began to meet to discuss ways to protest the Jim Crow laws.

and other new laws, the number of **convicts** at state prisons increased from less than 300 people to more than 1,000. Also in the state of Mississippi, the practice of the convict the lease system was started. The government would lease out convicts as laborers and receive payment for their work. Almost all of these convicts were African Americans. Both men and women were subjected to terrible conditions in work camps. The death rate in these camps was eight to eighteen percent.

Quick Facts

Court challenges to the Jim Crow laws were unsuccessful. In 1896, an African American man, Homer Plessy, was jailed for sitting in a train car of the East Louisiana Railroad that was intended for people of European ancestry.

The issue of segregation remained unsuccessfully challenged until the *Brown v. Board of Education* decision in 1954, when the Supreme Court ruled that racial segregation of schools was unconstitutional.

End of the Dream

Defeated on many fronts, the Reconstruction plan was shut down by **prejudice** and racial discrimination.

Fading Northern Support

The Civil War took a huge toll on Americans, and they were weary of the continued struggle of African Americans in the South. African American supporters in the Northern states were slowly losing sympathy for the African American fight for civil rights. News headlines of southern violence and corruption were losing their impact. This, along with an economic depression, shifted focus away from African Americans and their fight for civil rights and equality.

The Final Injustice

Reconstruction came to its official end when the southern states **codified** laws to enforce segregation. The Civil Rights Bill of 1875 prevented segregation in public facilities, but the law was struck down in 1883 by the Supreme Court. On October 15, the Supreme Court declared the Civil Rights Act of 1875 unconstitutional.

The court stated that the Fourteenth Amendment forbade states, but not citizens, from discriminating.

Booker T. Washington was an abolitionist who believed African Americans should not protest inequality but gain equality through hard work and patience.

Resistance

Organizations were created to fight segregation and violence against African Americans. One of the groups, the Afro-American League, was formed in January 25, 1890. However, after three years, the organization ran out of money and was forced to disband. In September 1898, a new group formed called National Afro-American Council. This council was the first nationwide civil rights group in the United States. Led by A.M.E. Zion Bishop Alexander Walters, membership included African American professionals and academics.

Niagara Movement

Frustrated by the restrictions of Jim Crow laws on African Americans, and the ideas presented by leaders such as Booker T. Washington, a group of **activists** met in 1905. Twenty-nine men formed a delegation, that hoped to create a militant opposition to Booker T. Washington's policies.

Led by W.E.B. Du Bois and William Monroe Trotter, this opposition group met at Niagara Falls to discuss issues of civil rights and fighting prejudicial laws. The meeting was planned to take place on the American side of the falls, but members of the group were refused hotel rooms because of their race. They moved the meeting to the Canadian side of the falls. The movement, later called the Niagara Movement, achieved a few small successes before it was disbanded in 1911.

Tunis Campbell

African American minister and visionary Tunis Campbell saw the period of Reconstruction as a chance to uplift African Americans in the South. He was part of a plan to create a new life for African Americans who were homeless after the Civil War. The new community he planned was self-sufficient and fulfilled the promises of Reconstruction.

Early Beginnings

Born 1812 in Middlebrook, New Jersey, Tunis Gulic Campbell was one of 10 children. At the age of five, Tunis began his education at an Episcopal school in Babylon, New York, on Long Island. At first, he trained to serve as a missionary in Liberia, Africa, but Tunis opposed leaving the United States. After converting to Methodism, he started to lecture on many issues, including slavery.

Reconstruction

As the Union army swept through the South, the homeless and landless situation of African Americans called

Fearing for their safety, many freed slaves fled the south for safety behind the Union army lines.

for action. A proposal to provide African American freedmen fertile land on the islands off the coast of Georgia was initiated. News of the land give away spread throughout the South, and African Americans came to own land. The plan to grant refugees 40 acres and a mule was put into action.

A community was established with Tunis at the head of local government. Long-term goals included economic and political self-sufficiency. However, former landowners learned of the plan and pushed President Johnson to return the land to southerners of European ancestry. The president complied and removed Tunis from his post in 1866.

Tunis campaigned in Georgia for the state Senate. He won a seat, but the majority of the Senate worked to remove Tunis and other African Americans from office. In 1868, 32 African Americans lost their seats. However, Congress intervened and the African American senators returned to the Senate.

Tunis shifted his focus to local politics, where he believed he could have a greater impact on people's lives. As a justice of the peace, Tunis encouraged African Americans to make sure that any labor contracts they signed were fair. This mandate brought Tunis many enemies, who tried to have him removed from his post. They succeeded, and Tunis was convicted of wrongdoing in office. At the age of 64, he was sent to a forced labor camp to serve his sentence. After a year, Tunis was released and moved his family to the North.

Inspiring Change

Tunis represented the ideals that characterized the Reconstruction period. He spent his last years doing missionary work for the African Methodist Episcopal Church in Boston. He died there in 1891. Tunis helped build an environment of reform and change that gave power to the African American community.

Leading Man

Tunis Campbell began his work life in the hotel industry. He worked from 1832 to 1845 as a hotel steward in New York City. At the Howard Hotel, Tunis worked as principal waiter. During this time, Tunis developed a drill for waiters that greatly increased efficiency. The method was so successful that Tunis wrote a guide explaining how it worked. It was published in 1848. This guide was a standard for hotel management because it included instruction and helpful tips for hotel keepers, head waiters, and housekeepers. The guide was the first book of its kind published in America.

A New Hope

African Americans were part of a decade of Reconstruction that has inspired generations of activists to continue the quest for civil rights. The achievements of Reconstruction, including constitutional amendments and improvements in education, created the basis for the Civil Rights Movement of the twentieth century.

African Americans leaders of the Reconstruction era tried to define what freedom meant to them and their community. These expressions continued to create a desire for equality for many generations.

Leading Change

For the first time, the Black Laws of the turn of the nineteenth century were directly challenged during the Civil War protests of the 1950s and 1960s. Rosa Parks effectively beat down the segregation laws by refusing to sit in the African American section of a public bus. African American civil rights protesters and their supporters marched for fair and equal treatment

The Civil Rights Movement created new attitudes and opportunities. African Americans and people of European ancestry began to understand and respect each other.

under the law. Their voices were heard, and another new era began for African Americans.

The Fight for Change Continues

Through the 1980s, 1990s, and today, many African Americans have worked toward equality and freedom for themselves and people of all races. African Americans serve in all areas of the United States military and within all ranks. Historians continue to discover new layers of African American history and learn more about the people who were absent from official histories, such as slaves, women, and children.

Movies, such as *Go Tell it on the Mountain*, *The Color Purple*, and *Roots*, portray life for African Americans in the nineteenth century. The producers and actors in these features have broken down barriers by demonstrating how African Americans fought to gain their freedom.

TECHNOLOGY LINK
To learn more about African Americans who continue to strive for equal treatment, visit www.naacp.org

Timeline

1619: Africans are captured and brought to Jamestown, Virginia, to work as slaves.

1619

1807: Congress declares it illegal to bring slaves into the United States.

1831-1861: About 75,000 slaves escape by the Underground Railroad, a network that helped protect and hide escaped slaves so they could find freedom.

1861: The Civil War begins. One of the main issues behind the conflict is to determine if slavery should be allowed.

1909

1863: President Abraham Lincoln passes the Emancipation Proclamation, which legally frees all slaves.

1865: Congress passes the Thirteenth Amendment, which outlaws slavery.

1866: Congress passes the Civil Rights Act, which declares African Americans as citizens.

1881: The first Jim Crow Law is passed in Tennessee.

1896: In Plessy v. Ferguson, the Supreme Court rules that public places may be segregated as long as equal facilities are given to African Americans.

1909: The National Association for the Advancement of Colored People (NAACP) is formed.

1910-1920: During a period known as the Great Migration, about 500,000 African Americans move to northern states.

1861

1914: Marcus Garvey forms the Universal Negro Improvement Association in Jamaica. The group eventually opens branches in the United States.

1919: A series of violent events occur in response to the Great Migration. The period is known as "Red Summer" because of the hundreds of deaths that resulted from the violence.

1600   **1800**   **1850**   **1900**

1942: The Congress of Racial Equality (CORE) is started in Chicago.

1948: President Truman desegregates the army.

1954: In Brown v. Board of Education of Topeka, the Supreme Court rules against school segregation.

1955: The Montgomery Bus Boycott begins when Rosa Parks refuses to give up her seat to a passenger of European ancestry.

1957: A community in Little Rock, Arkansas opposes desegregation and plans a protest to prevent nine African American students from entering a school that was formerly for students of European ancestry. The African American students are later called "The Little Rock Nine."

1960: At a Woolworth's lunch counter in Greensboro, North Carolina, four African American college students hold the first sit-in.

1961: The Congress of Racial Equality (CORE) begins to organize Freedom Rides.

1963

1963: Martin Luther King, Jr. writes "Letter from a Birmingham Jail."

1964: Martin Luther King, Jr. is awarded the Nobel Peace Prize.

1965: Malcolm X is assassinated in New York.

1983: Astronaut Guion "Guy" S. Bluford, Jr., becomes the first African American in space, flying aboard the space shuttle *Challenger*.

1985: Philadelphia State Police bomb a house in Philadelphia occupied by an African American activist organization, MOVE, killing 11 occupants and triggering a fire that destroyed a neighborhood and left more than 300 people homeless.

1986: Martin Luther King, Jr.'s birthday is made into a national holiday.

1989: General Colin L. Powell is the first African American to be named chair of the Joint Chiefs of Staff of the U.S. military.

1989: Oprah Winfrey becomes the first African American woman to host a nationally syndicated talk show.

2008: Barack Obama, a politician from Chicago's South Side, becomes the first African American to secure a major party nomination as a presidential candidate.

1961

2008

1950   1960   1980   2000

Activity

Writing Poetry

Writing poetry as a way to communicate ideas of protest is a creative way to shed light on a significant concept. Poetry is the expression of thoughts, ideas, and feelings into a blend of sound and imagery. Protest is expressing objection or disapproval to something a person is powerless to prevent. Protest poetry brings together this form of written expression with the passion of opposition.

You will need:

✓ a pen
✓ paper
✓ a dictionary
✓ access to the Internet

On a sheet of paper, write down a single statement about a problem or issue that you believe needs to be challenged. Create a concept map of words that are linked to your statement. Try to add at least five main words with three related words linked to them. These words can be used to express your thoughts and feelings about the issue. Now, write a poem using these words. Remember, there are many types of poems, and the words do not have to rhyme.

Now, you have now created a protest poem. Share your poem with people. Ask if they understood the thoughts and feelings you were hoping to express in the poem. Did the poem have impact? In what way?

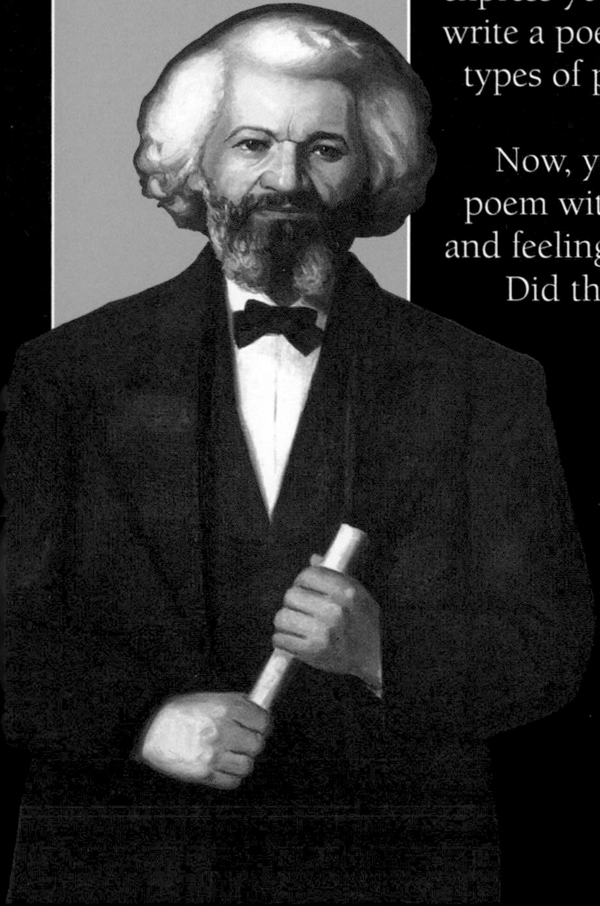

Test Your Knowledge

Q What was the title of Frances Ellen Watkins Harper's first collection of poems, and when was it published?

A *Autumn Leaves* was published in 1845

Q What was the first set of restrictive laws called that reduced the civil rights of African Americans during the 1860s?

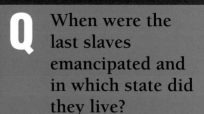

A The Black Codes

Q What was the name of the first African American owned and published newspaper?

A *The New Orleans Tribune*

Q What year was the Freedmen's Bureau established?

A 1865

Q What crime was Homer Plessy charged with?

A breaking the segregation law

Q When were the last slaves emancipated and in which state did they live?

A Slaves in Texas received the news they were free two months after the Civil War ended on June 19, 1865.

Further Research

Books

Learn more about Reconstruction by reading the following books.

Asim, Jabari. *The Road to Freedom: A Story of the Reconstruction, Jamestown's American Portraits.* Grand Rapids, Michigan. School Specialty Publishing, 2004.

Bolden, Tonya. *Cause: Reconstruction America 1863-1877.* New York, New York. Knopf Books for Young Readers, 2005.

Websites

To learn more about African American History and Culture, visit **www.pbs.org/wnet/aaworld/index.html**

To learn more about Reconstruction, visit **http://memory.loc.gov/ammem/aaohtml/exhibit/aopart5.html**.

Glossary

abolish: to do away with

abolitionists: person who is against slavery

activists: people who work toward solutions to social problems

amendments: further clarification of statutes in the Constitution

amnesty: a pardon, or forgiveness, given by a government

assassinated: killed by a surprise or secret attack

census: a count of people living in a select area

citizenship: the criteria for belonging to a nation

civil rights: freedoms and responsibilities of a citizen

codified: classified and organized into a legal code

colonization: migration of people of one country into another to establish a settlement

Confederate: member state of the alliance that separated from the Union states

Congress: national legislative organization of the United States

convicts: people who are found guilty of a crime

democratic: a nation where all citizens can cast a vote

enfranchisement: meeting all of the requirements to vote

fugitive: a person running from authority

indentured: a contract by which one person is made to work for another for a stated period

institution: an official and accepted authority

liberty: personal and societal freedoms

lynching: taking people from their home and beating or killing them in a public display

migration: movement of individuals from one place to another

orator: a public speaker especially good at addressing large crowds

paramilitary: a group that has a military structure but is not part of a nation's armed forces

periodical: a journal or newspaper that is published at regular intervals

pole tax: a tax imposed on every adult in a community

prejudice: hostility toward a person or group of people based on race or origin

Quaker: a religious sect that advocated abolition and equality of all races

racism: judgements about people based on their race

ratified: approved and enacted

segregation: legal separation between people based on race or gender

self-sufficient: to be independent of outside support

sharecrop: an agreement to lease farmland by giving part of crop to the landowner

suffrage: a women's movement to gain the right of citizenship and to vote

supremacist: a person who believes that people of European ancestry should control all others

Union: states that remained loyal to the federal government

vigilantism: when a person or group decides to punish criminals, without concern for the law

Index

abolition 17, 29
African American
    Church 29
African Methodist Episcopal
    Church 21, 39

Black Codes 12, 13, 21, 27,
    30, 45

Campbell, Tunis 38, 39
Canada 17, 23
churches 7, 24, 29, 33, 34
Civil War 5, 7, 9, 11, 12, 13,
    14, 15, 18, 21, 22, 23, 24,
    27, 28, 33, 36, 38, 40,
    42, 45

Douglass, Frederick 10, 13

Emancipation Proclamation
    10, 11, 12, 22, 42

Fifteenth Amendment 13,
    20, 30, 31
First African Baptist Church 29
Fourteenth Amendment 13, 37
Freedmen's Bureau 18, 19, 24,
    25, 26, 29, 45
Fugitive Slave Law 17

Gettysburg Address 9

Howard University 25

Johnson, Andrew 5, 19, 27,
30, 38

Kansas 22, 23

Liberia 23, 38
Lincoln, Abraham 5, 7, 9, 10,
    13, 19, 26, 30, 42
New Orleans Tribune, The
    25, 45
Niagara Movement 37

Plessy, Homer 35, 42, 45

Revels, Hiram 21

segregation 27, 34, 35, 36, 37,
    40, 43, 45
slavery 5, 6, 7, 9, 10, 11, 12,
    13, 22, 23, 29, 30, 38, 42
South Carolina 6, 9
Spelman College 25

Thirteenth Amendment 12,
    13, 42
troops 14, 18, 26, 31

Watkins Harper, Frances Ellen
    17, 45